big sky

country

a view of paradise

THE BEST OF MONTANA, NORTH DAKOTA, WYOMING, AND IDAHO

Photographs by Michael Melford

With an introduction by WILLIAM KITTREDGE

RIZZOLI

First published in the United States of America in 1996 by
Rizzoli International Publications, Inc.
300 Park Avenue South
New York, NY 10010

Library of Congress Cataloging-in-Publication Data

Melford, Michael.
Big sky country : a view of paradise : the best of Montana, North Dakota, Wyoming, and Idaho /
photographs by Michael Melford ; introduction by William Kittredge.
p. cm.
ISBN 0-8478-1964-7 (HC)
1. West (U.S.)—Pictorial works. 2. West (U.S.)—Description and travel. 3. Montana—Pictorial works.
4. North Dakota—Pictorial works. 5. Wyoming—Pictorial works. 6. Idaho—Pictorial works. I. Title.

F590.7.M45 1996
978—dc20   96-16309
                                                                              CIP

Excerpts accompanying the photographs are taken from the following sources:

From ALDER GULCH IN 1863 by Mary Ronan as published in
FRONTIER WOMAN: THE STORY OF MARY RONAN, AS TOLD TO MARGARET RONAN (1973).
Used with permission of the University of Montana.

From AUDUBON AND HIS JOURNALS by John James Audubon and edited by Maria Audubon,
as published in 1960 by Dover Publications, Inc.. Used with permission of Dover Publications, Inc.

From BIG ROCK CANDY MOUNTAIN by Wallace Stegner. Copyright 1938, 1940, 1942, 1943 by Wallace Stegner.
Used by permission of Doubleday, a division of Bantam Doubleday Dell Publishing Group, Inc.

Excerpt from THE BIG SKY. Copyright (c) 1947, renewed 1974 by A.B. Guthrie, Jr.
Reprinted by permission of Houghton Mifflin Company. All rights reserved.

From HOMESTEAD DAYS by Pearl Price Robertson as published in THE FRONTIER magazine (1933).
Used with permission of the University of Montana.

From "MY COUNTRY AS TOLD TO ROBERT CAMBELL" by Arapooish, Chief of the Crows as published in
CONTRIBUTIONS OF THE HISTORICAL SOCIETY OF MONTANA, Volume 9 (1923).
Used with permission of the Montana Historical Society Press.

From UBET by John R. Barrows as published in 1934. Used with permission of The Caxton Printers, Ltd.

From WILDERNESS KINGDOM: INDIAN LIFE IN THE ROCKY MOUNTAINS: 1840–1847 by Nicolas Point, S.J.
Copyright (c) 1967 by Nicholas Point, S.J. Reprinted by permission of Henry Holt and Co., Inc.

Half-title page: Farm, Bynum, Montana
Opposite: Full moon setting over Grand Teton, Grand Teton National Park.

Designed by David Larkin
Typographic design by Meredith Miller

PRINTED IN ITALY

There is only one question:
How to love this world.
                    from SPRING *by Mary Oliver*

The great moon was more silvery than white in the luminous blue of an early summer
sky over the Tetons. Hungover and semi-heartbroken when I woke at sun-up in Jackson,
Wyoming, I'd gotten out of town in a hurry, before any true sense of my own isolation
could come catch me.

It was a getaway that didn't work. Alongside Teton Lake, leaning against the fender of
my yellow Toyota, studying the daylight moon, I was frightened to almost breathless death.
This was what was, and I was alone in its vicinity, under its gaze. Much as I wanted to love
the silence and light, that moon was an intimation of unfathomable dooms and infinities.

My friend Jack Turner, who is a sort of thinking man's climbing guide, tells of lying
on his back on top of the highest peak in the Tetons of a morning and seeing flashes of
white, which turned out to be pelicans circling a mile above him at some great elevation,
sporting in the glory of things so far as anyone could tell. Which is a prime way of curing
ourselves of that panic which inhabits the untethered soul: sporting.

Maybe, without my knowing, that morning, pelicans were up there playing as I
shivered and hit the road for Missoula.

As the Chuang-tzu puts it:

...never consent to be one thing alone.

A tall man with an orange-stained mustache said something to the effect that
nobody knew how mean winter could be until they had tried cowboying in Montana.
He told of men riding horses and motorcycles into country bars. He said anybody tough
enough to survive in Montana was liable to do just any damned thing they could think of.

Those stories stayed with me on my first trip to the northern Rockies, through
Spokane and the Idaho Panhandle and the miner's towns like Kellogg and Wallace (the
second-floor downtown bordellos were still open in those days). I was looking for what I
took to be a genuine world to inhabit. I wanted to turn out to be someone I understood
and could stand. It was a romantic but not entirely bad idea that seems commonplace in
the mountain West these days. It's a story a lot of people are acting out.

Heading up Lookout Pass into Montana I studied ranch buildings in the valley
below, set in the edges of the timber and looking to be remnants from the sort of medieval
world I'd grown up in, slower and simpler days before World War II when country people
I knew revered good horses and killed their beef at home, by hand, and gathered greens
from the garden in summertime.

The northern Rockies seemed like a sweet prelapsarian place, an undiscovered land, thick with secrets no one bothered to keep. A woman I know told me about growing up in a shack on the flats west of Missoula alongside the Clark Fork River, and the way her people would dynamite fish in the fall. She and her brothers and sisters would gather those trout and suckers from a rowboat with nets. Their family would live the winter off fish canned in glass jars.

She told me this to emphasize that she was a native, and that my elegant catch-and-release fly-fishing world could go piss up a rope so far as she was concerned, and why she wasn't thrilled when upscale Missoula restaurants began featuring fresh salmon flown in every day from Seattle. She'd eaten enough fish for a lifetime. It was an honest way of speaking by a woman who valued her origins.

Sammy Thompson's Eastgate Liquor Lounge and Trail's End Tavern in Missoula were my social centers. Sammy was a generous man who grew up tending bars in the legendary railroad and ranchhand taverns along Woody Street in Missoula (they where gone by the time I got to town), a stockcar racing and speedboat man.

Showing off for a woman, running his speedboat hard as it would go under summertime stars over Flathead Lake, Sammy hit a drifting log. The speedboat overturned. The woman said they hung on to that floating speedboat until sun-up. Then Sammy slid underneath.

Sammy's funeral wasn't anything I wanted to know about. I felt like somebody had torn up the dance floor. Maybe they had. Maybe it was the man in the moon.

But springtime alleyways all over town were thick with blossoming clumps of purple and lilac and people on their way to work stopped on the street to spend time talking to the mayor (they still do). We left our doors unlocked. "Them locks," somebody told me, "only keep out the honest people."

So I didn't entirely despair; I tried to discover reasons for taking care. Again, it seems to be a common concern in the West these days.

One way of enlarging ourselves is the educational comedy of hitting the road. It's a particularly American form, sometimes called "The Traveling Cure," which has been a communal enterprise in the West since the fur trappers and wagon trains. Think of Huck Finn heading out for territory, Hemingway in Spain and Africa, Willie Nelson and all those cowboy beatniks heading down those lonesome highways. Such goings can be understood as ways of seeking out the freedom to be whatever you can manage.

North of Missoula, where Highway 93 crests along the southern boundary of the National Bison Range, you all at once are witness to the vast weave of high rock walls which are the Mission Mountains hanging like a curtain on the eastern horizon.

In October, the mountains are dusted with snow while hayfields in the valley below remain green even if the willows and cottonwood along Post Creek are turning red. That's how it was when I saw it in 1969, my first autumn in Montana. You might think that this is a paradise where we could have made our stand if we'd had any sense.

But that valley is not a white man's paradise for the taking. It's the heart of the 1.25 million acre Flathead Indian Reservation, and governed by the Confederated Salish and Kootenai Tribes, a sovereign nation inside the United States. Everywhere in the West, as we know, was Indian country.

History has been ferociously sad for Native American people, but on the Flathead Reservation the tribes are educating their children and governing themselves, taking charge of their own future with what looks to be wisdom and restraint.

On Good Friday some of us used to visit the red brick cathedral in the reservation town of St. Ignatius, at the foot of the Mission Mountains. Native people would chant the liturgy in Salish, and that night carry a wooden approximation of Christ to outdoor bonfires marking the stations of the cross. We didn't believe in their prayers; we wondered if they did, actually. We stopped going, maybe because we were unsettled by the fact that we saw our religious situation reflected in the mirror of theirs. We turn out to be alike in the most profound ways.

In the summer of 1970 Jim Crumley leased a cabin near Polebridge, just across the north fork of the Flathead River from Glacier Park. Jim was supposed to be working on his second novel, but most of the time he was on his motorcycle, into the curves he said, and he had lots of company. In June some of us drove the Going-to-the-Sun Road across the mountainous spine of Glacier Park just before it was closed by summer snow.

The interior of Glacier is a kingdom of crystalline lakes beneath knife-edged precipitous cirque walls of rock carved over millennia by glaciers, of hanging icefields and waterfalls and tiny dark gorges cut by the rushing waters. On that afternoon reefs of misty clouds hung below us against the dark evergreen slopes. All our sweet chatter turned silent.

The honking world had been so quickly transformed; it had gone utterly distant from anything we ordinarily experienced and yet it was absolutely recognizable, forgotten and intricate. It was like recalling a dream of a place where we played as children, swirling around us.

Later that summer we walked in. In scrubby primordial timber off the trail to Bowman Lake, flecked with shadows and sunlight, I stepped from one to another great platter-shaped and luridly colored mushroom, crushing them. It was like walking on stones across water. Then I killed a grouse with a lucky stone's throw (we cooked it primitively, impaled on a green branch along with trout).

That night we got stoned, having traded part of our catch to some fellows down the lake who had forgotten their food but remembered to bring a grocery sack stuffed with smoking materials, and we sipped at shots from one of our bottles of whiskey, and talked about the chance of venturing into willows along the creek in search of trout, and finding a grizzly. We were at least self-aware enough to wonder if this was the way Hemingway thought—the short happy life—and laughed and laughed and laughed.

Later I woke to behold moonlight in a long wash across the stillness of the lake. What if this, I thought, was the last thing you ever saw? In the morning we never mentioned the chance of confronting bears; we stayed out of the willows, trolling open water along the edge of the lake from a makeshift raft held together by bailing wire and an old pair of suspenders.

On a warm summer night a few years later Mary Pat Mahoney, a young friend, was dragged from her tent in a Glacier campground, killed, and partways eaten. I was consumed with anger more than sorrow and wondered why. I would wake in the night and think of vengeance. Finally I was driven to write a story called "We Are Not In This Together." Before the writing was done I had to acknowledge that the best revenge was going on with your days, peacefulness while pursuing your own chances.

There's a Native American Bear Mother story in which a woman is stolen away from her people to live with a bear. She gives birth to twins who are half human and half bear. When the Bear Husband is killed by the woman's brothers her sons take off their bear coats and—because they are willing to recognize the sacredness of bears—they become great hunters. The story is a way traditional people acknowledge kindship with animals, who are often thought of as making us the gift of their lives so that we may survive.

It is a story of death and renewal, vanishing and coming back from a long winter of hibernation (some enactment of sacred return may have been the earliest religious story), and of our irrevocable connection to the rhythms of what we call nature.

Stories hold us together, in ourselves, and with one another. We use them to reimagine ourselves, the most necessary art. In the Bob Marshall Wilderness with Annick Smith (we've been companions in this transit for a long time) I stood beside horses amid plumes of beargrass below the high rocky escarpment along the Continental Divide which is called the Chinese Wall. Our guide told of rutting elk sounding off for one another in autumn, when the larch have turned golden and their needles have fallen. Experts say there are more elk in that country than when Lewis and Clark made their way up the Missouri, just to the east, in 1805. We vowed to be back, not to hunt but with the intent of being witness. We have never gone there again, not so far. The possibility is like money in the bank.

Annick and I walked in four or five miles to Wall Lake in British Columbia, just out of Waterton Park, at the foot of a great curving, vertical wall of stone with mid-summer ice at the top. The next morning we saw a wolverine—a creature that's been almost exterminated from tame world. It resembled a reddish dark badger, implacable, untamable, and almost feverish in the quick absolute way it went about foraging on a gravel bar near the water. It was there, then aware of us, and gone.

Everything alive is not bent to our will. I never expect to see another wolverine. That encounter will stay with me; it was good for my soul to encounter a creature so utterly unavailable to our agendas, to see that such a way of going at life was still possible.

These memories move in my brain like little fires, reigniting the knowledge that the electricities of this world are in fact always flowing through us like blood. We are inescapably part of every lightning storm, mushroom, and bear, grizzly or not, wedded as can be, like trout in the dazzling stream of what is.

For years it was a tradition. On a bright Sunday morning in mid-June, wild roses blooming along the fencelines through the meadows, we'd drive upstream along the Big Blackfoot River (which was not the river filmed in *A River Runs Through It*, even though it's the river where Norman Maclean's brother Paul did his magical fishing). Beyond the Continental Divide we were into the rolling glaciated country along the Rockies Front, short grass prairies reaching away to the east for a thousand miles.

We were heading for the rodeo in the village of Augusta, set in a perfect country way among cottonwood along the Sun River. We drank in the darkness of taverns, walked three or four hundred yards through light and shadow under the trees, and found the rodeo grounds, out in the sunlight where western music was playing on the public address system. Country men and women were unloading their roping horses from aluminum trailers and we ate some hot dogs and bought beer to load our cooler and made our way to seats right near the chutes, where the bellowing and stink and cursing and laughter and flying mud and snot and the odor of piss were thick around us. World-class riders were landing their little airplanes out in the meadows, riding their bucking horses out of the chutes, then flying again to make some other show that night, maybe down in Cody, Wyoming. People I traveled with took the whole thing to be a day at the circus.

The old ways become picturesque and commercial, commodified. The bull riders and team ropers and cowboy poets are taken to be entertainers just as outlanders are taken to be tourists, with pockets full of money, willing to buy but at the same time seriously condescending to locals. It is a recipe for misunderstanding which colors a lot of transactions in the West.

What so many are looking for, as I understand it, is some connection of the old resolute life before the invention of incessant irony. A friend called it "actual time." Before the world went virtual. But rodeo is not a good place to look, if you're just traveling and not in the competition. The cowboy world, when it goes public, is pretty much a media invention, the sort of thing we see everywhere, glitz and images for sale. "The bigger the hat," one bowlegged fellow said to me, grinning and shaking his head and spitting snoose, "the smaller the ranch."

10

The way I like to practice traveling these days is to head out through the distance and its towns with no destination. My old pal Richard Hugo, an experienced survivor of multiple dislocations who helped a lot of us define our lives in the northern Rockies, was the poet laureate of such going.

Dick came from Seattle at the age of forty to teach at the University of Montana. Soon his wife left. Dick was alone, at least as he understood it, with an endlessness of time and his automobiles. Dick came to specialize in Buick convertibles, so he could run his new territories with the top down on sunny days, good jazz on the radio, looking for a town where he could spend an evening in the tavern in conversation with strangers, hoping for thoughts to trigger a poem while the talked drifted. Every so often you luck into gold.

The last stanza of "Driving Montana" is one of our defining texts in the northern Rockies:

> *Tomorrow will open again, the sky wide*
> *as the mouth of a wild girl, friable*
> *clouds you lose yourself to. You are lost*
> *in miles of land without people, without*
> *one fear of being found....*

Dead ends can be forgotten amid glories.

Up north of Augusta, at a property owned by the Nature Conservancy, a wildlands fen just below the Rockies Front where the grizzlies still come out on the plains as they did before the white men came, a place called the Pine Butte Swamp, local people held a gathering in honor of the novelist Bud Guthrie in October of 1993. Bud was very old, clearly dying, a man who devoted much of his last energies to the preservation of what remnants of the natural world remained in the country where he had mostly lived.

Men and women Guthrie had lived among for decades spoke to the particularities of their friendships. Then we drove out along the Teton River, country Bud wrote about in *The Big Sky* as a ruined paradise. In 1830 an old trapper says, "Gone, by God, and naught to care savin' some of us who seen'er new."

"God, she was purty onc't," that man said.

It still was. We didn't know what we had missed. Perhaps the country was tracked and roaded, but it was not so far as we could see particularly spoiled. Bud's storytelling helped us see it not as ruined but laid with histories.

Stories helped us understand what had happened in that long Montana valley where October snow was blowing down from the mountains through the twilight. Stories helped us live with own fragilities as we watched Bud and his old friends take stock and breathe the joys of fellowship for close to the last time in the Choteau country that afternoon. We understood that our turn was coming, sooner than might be hoped, and that we ought to prepare, if such preparations are possible.

Exactly like history, stories accumulate, and drive us to be what we are. And there are places where they intersect and congregate, like the Great Falls of the Missouri, seventy or so miles east of the Rockies Front, a series of shelfs where the river drops from the highlands to the plains.

The Missouri was the main interior waterway to the West, as much a northwest passage as existed, and for so long the route of travel which connected the northern Rockies to St. Louis, New Orleans, the sea, and civilizations like France and England.

On Thursday, June 13, 1805, Meriwether Lewis sat above the falls and wrote that they were "the grandest sight I ever beheld." A grizzly chased Lewis into the river the next day, and the expedition spent a month making an eighteen mile portage around the falls in country thick with prickly pear cactus, but danger and difficulty were not the message.

The journals kept by Lewis and Clark are among our defining documents in America, like *Leaves of Grass* or Lincoln's address at Gettysburg; they tell us to go toward possibility.

Just upstream from the falls, in the 1880s, a visionary named Paris Gibson laid out an ideal community he called Great Falls. He planted thousands of tiny oak and elm along avenues staked across the prairies, and hired men to go out at dawn and water them from wagon-loads of barrels filled out of the Missouri. Charlie Russell set up his log cabin studio on one of those avenues. These days it's a district of aging rich-man houses shaded by those enormous trees.

In 1887 the Great Northern Railroad arrived; Black Eagle, the first of four hydro-electric dams built on the falls, was completed in 1890; Anaconda Company set up their first copper reduction plant in 1892. Great Falls is a place where a lot of economic dreams worked out, at least for a while.

A dozen years ago I stood at the top of the Ulm Pishkun, a cliff just north of the Missouri, maybe a dozen miles west of Great Falls, where tribesmen once drove stampeding bison to their death (it was a way of hunting). On the eastern horizon the great abandoned brick smoke stack over the Anaconda Company refinery towered into the clear morning. To the west I could see the snowy peaks of the "shining mountains" on the Rockies Front, looking just as they did when Lewis and Clark saw them. Here, I thought, here's our history of dreams in this part of the world.

But not entirely, by a long shot.

The vast dry land farming country locals call the "Golden Triangle," enormous strips of fallow ground and wheatland which run over the plains to the horizon, and on, begins north of Great Falls. Distances between the little towns clustered at the foot of the towering grain elevators on the "high-line" along the Great Northern tracks were dictated by concerns about getting the crops to market. This is the land of windbreaks beside white-painted farmsteads, enormous four-wheel-drive diesel tractors and land-poor millionaires with serious cash flow problems (a viable wheat farm on these plains is worth a million anyway).

Out on those plains we find ourselves wondering about the rewards of freedom which led people to stick it out through blistering summers and blizzard winters, raising children on places where the nearest doctor was maybe fifty snow-drifted miles away.

The isolation is hardest to deal with, even today, for people who can afford all the electronic connection to media there is. Sometimes you need to get into town, in person.

In Richard Ford's story "Communist," a young man, recalling a cold afternoon spent hunting geese on one of the lakes that fill shallow depressions left by glaciers in this country, says "...I looked toward the Highwood Mountains twenty miles away, half in snow and half dark blue at the bottom. I could see the little town of Floweree then, looking shabby and dimly lighted in the distance. A red bar sign shone. A car moved slowly away from the scattered buildings." He hears the geese on the lake, thousands of them, before he can see them, a sound "...that made your chest rise and your shoulders tighten with expectancy. It was a sound that to make you feel separate from it and everything else, as if you were of no importance in the grand scheme of things."

That sense of separation can overwhelm you. Life in the northern Rockies or on plains often seems to go on in a way not much connected to the doings of the so-called "Great World." Ambitious young people leave early and never go home for more than a few days at Christmas. Many of the people who stay develop a deep mistrust of anything happening beyond their emotional horizon. It is a way of being dysfunctional.

People like James Welch, the Blackfeet/Gros Ventre writer who did some of his growing up near the Milk River west of Harlem, are rare and invaluable. In his first novel, *Winter in the Blood*, Welch took on those feelings, and showed us a young man finding his way beyond them into the slow rhythms involved in connecting to his people and himself amid such distances. It is a supremely *useful* book for people in the northern West, both Native Americans and whites. Any life, anywhere, we see, can be in ways rewarding, if we allow, if we have imagination enough.

"Some people," his young man says in *Winter in the Blood*, "will never know how pleasant it is to be distant in a clean rain, the driving rain of a summer storm. It's not like you'd expect, nothing like you'd expect." Maybe it's all in learning to see the splendor of what you have.

Wallace Stegner spent some of his boyhood, in the early days of this century, in the Cypress Hills on the border between Montana and Saskatchewan. In *The Big Rock Candy Mountain* he writes, "They could stand quietly in the door and watch the good rain come, the front of it like a wall and the wind ahead of it stirring up dust, until it reached them and drenched the bare packed earth of the yard, and the ground smoked under it's feet, and darkened, and ran with little streams . . . ." The good rain: reasons for loving this world.

Out on these plains, hundreds of miles east of the shining mountains, we are in what can be thought of as "The Land of Little Kingdoms," with hours of nothing but territory between them—Hutterite colonies, and cowboy towns like Miles City, and homesteader towns like Ryegate—you can drive north from Ryegate to the Snowy Mountains, into windy country where the settlement boom came before World War I and pass one abandoned homestead after another. Houses and barns lean with the wind, shingles mostly blown away. This is the land of ICBM silos.

This country is talked about as a possible "Buffalo Commons," a preserve devoted to global biodiversity if not for the few endlessly stubborn settlers who remain. It would be larger than Ohio.

After driving the prairies for hours, Annick and I walked into a motel in Jordan, Montana, a town of about six hundred souls south of the great reservoir backed up behind the Fort Peck Dam. The clerk asked "Are you paleontologists?" Jordan, it turns out, is where bone hunters headquarter when they're out searching the clay-bank badlands washs above the Missouri for another skeleton of *Tyrannosaurus Rex*. Out on these plains we are continually in touch with infinities.

Militia crusaders have taken to holing up in the vicinity of Jordan. Locals wish they'd go away, but tolerate them. Settlers on the plains have a long history of political extremism. No one gets too excited so long as there's no serious trouble.

Radicalism in this part of the world started with the socialist Non-Partisan League in North Dakota, farmers calling for state-owned grain elevators and a state-owned bank. In 1918 the Non-Partisan League set up a newspaper called *Producer's News* in Plentywood, in the northeastern corner of Montana. After 1920 many of the maybe three thousand voters in Sheridan County were Communists; they ran the county for a few years; in 1930 about five hundred citizens were still voting the straight Communist Party ticket.

It was another attempt at kingdom, enterprises that can be thought of as working toward the creation of a paradise, a try at making the world go your way. It is one of our oldest and most honorable traditions in America.

But maybe those plains were already a paradise. We see great herds of buffalo running in a film like *Dances With Wolves*, and can't articulate reasons why we are so moved. By the 1890s the buffalo were mostly gone from the plains. The Crow warrior Two Leggings said, "Nothing happened after that. We just lived . . . . There is nothing more to tell."

To try understanding what it was like to come upriver on the Missouri in the 1830s and 1840s, study the art of George Catlin and Karl Bodmer, who were there, look into Catlin's journals and Audubon's *Missouri River Journals*. Read the contemporary accounts in Ian Frazier's *Great Plains* and Merrill Gilfillan's *Magpie Rising* and Barry

Lopez's *Winter Count.* If you should go there in the summertime, driving west through bright fields of sunflowers in North Dakota, travel with those books, and go slow. You will find yourself in touch with lost glories that can break your heart; loss, as we know, is always part of love.

The story of John Colter's several hundred mile walk is another of our defining legends in the northern West. The autumn and winter of 1807-08, through country no known white man had yet seen, Colter went from Fort Lisa, at the junction of the Bighorn River and the Yellowstone, down to Jackson Hole and the far side of the Tetons, and back through the spectacles of what would be Yellowstone Park. I want to think he was running on wisdom, and not simple-minded courage; I want to think his isolation was something he accepted as a version of what we always have. I like to think Colter loved his chance to be where he was.

Think of Yellowstone in winter, seven thousand seven hundred feet in elevation at the lake, the nighttime lows thirty and forty below, snows a dozen feet in depth, and the hot sulfur springs boiling up, the grass still green beside them, down there in the warm enclosure with the drifted snow high above your head.

Think of early spring, bison wandering through the mist near the steaming river where the trumpeter swans glide on glassy ponds. Colter had been with Lewis and Clark as they climbed the long grade to Lemhi Pass, on the Continental Divide, imagining the beginnings of the great River Columbia, an easy route to the Pacific, might lie on the other side. Instead they saw the blue mountains of what is now central Idaho, range after range.

John Colter knew there was no easy way out. I like to think he might have studied a full daylight moon over the Tetons, as I did more than a hundred and eighty years later, and felt he was as close to the sweet center of things as he would ever need to be, and privileged.

William Kittredge

Storm clouds, Theodore Roosevelt National Park, North Dakota.

Opposite: Early morning fog along the Snake River, Grand Teton National Park, Wyoming.

Missouri River, Theodore Roosevelt National Park, North Dakota.

The Crow country is exactly in the right place.

It has snowy mountains and sunny plains,

all kinds of climates and good things for every season.

When the summer heats scorch the prairies,

you can draw up under the mountains,

where the air is sweet and cool,

the grass fresh, and the bright streams

come tumbling out of the snowbanks...

The Crow country is exactly in the right place.

Everything good is to be found there.

There is no country like the Crow country.

Arapooish, Chief of the Crows

*Petrified tree trunk in the Petrified Forest, Theodore Roosevelt
National Park, North Dakota.*

Badlands, Theodore Roosevelt National Park.

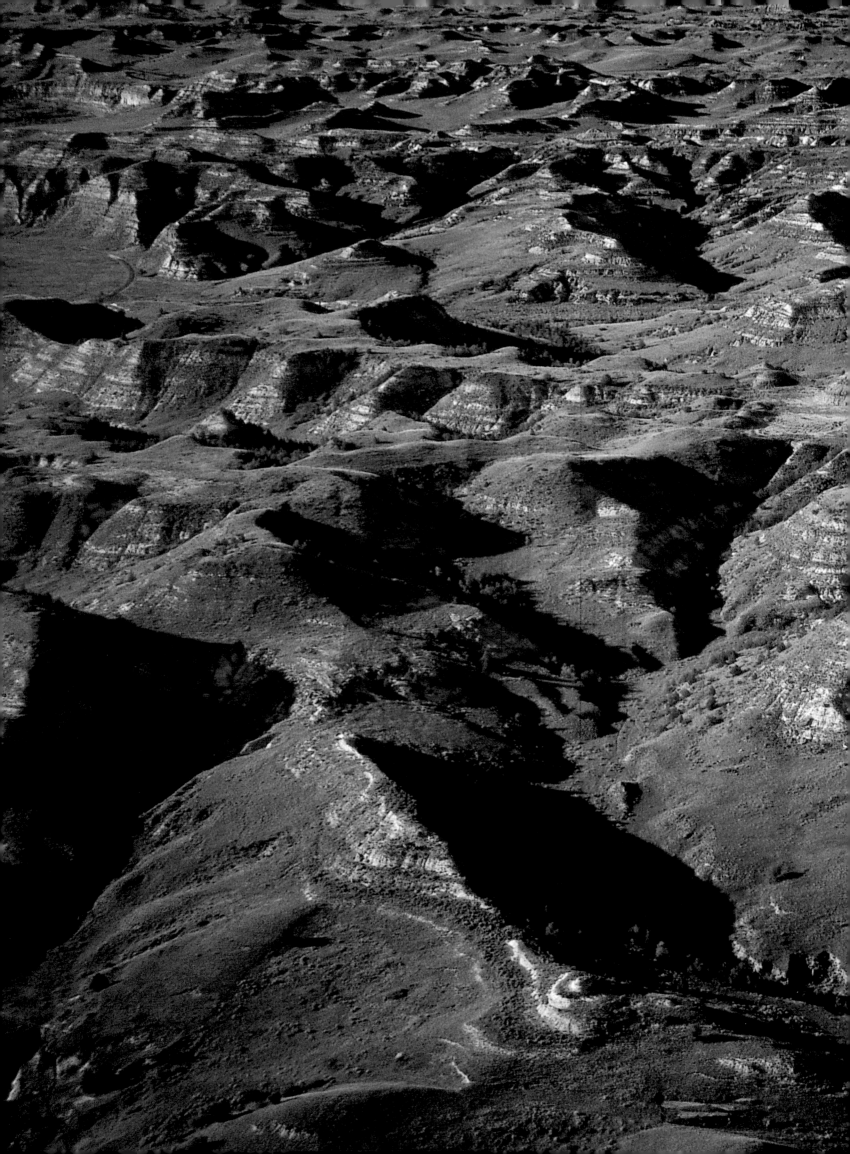

Bighorn Canyon, Montana.

In the autumn when your horses are fat

and strong from the mountain pastures

you can go down into the plains and hunt

the buffalo, or trap beaver on the streams.

And when winter comes on, you can take shelter

in the woody bottoms along the rivers;

there you will find buffalo meat

for yourselves and cottonwood bark for your horses,

or you may winter in the Wind River valley,

where there is salt weed in abundance.

Arapooish, Chief of the Crows

26

Clark Canyon Reservoir, Dillon, Montana.

Moonrise over Clark Canyon, Montana.

The interior of Glacier is a kingdom of crystalline lakes beneath knife-edged precipitous cirque walls of rock carved over millennia by glaciers, of hanging icefields and waterfalls and tiny dark gorges cut by the rushing waters.

From the Introduction

Lake McDonald, Glacier National Park, Montana.

First snow near Logan Pass, Glacier National Park, Montana.

Avalanche Gorge, Glacier National Park.

33

Rising Sun Trail, Little Chief Mountain,
Glacier National Park, Montana.

35

Beargrass at Haystack Creek,
Glacier National Park, Montana.

There were tall buttercups and blue flags in the valley.

Up Alder Gulch snow and timber lilies bloomed, wild roses

and syringa grew in sweet profusion and flowering currant bushes

invited canaries to alight and twitter. There were great patches

of moss-flowers with a scent and blossom like sweet-william.

And such forget-me-nots—larger and bluer and glossier

than any others I have ever seen. On the tumbled hills

among and over which the town straggled the primroses

made pink splotches in early spring; there the yellowbells

nodded and the bitterroots unfolded close to the ground

their perplexity of rose petals.

Mary Ronan. Alder Gulch in 1863

preceding pages:
Wild Goose Island, St. Mary Lake, Glacier National Park, Montana.

Medicine Rocks State Park, Eastern Montana.

Moonrise over sage, Cut Bank, Montana.

About the forks of the Missouri is a fine country;

good water, good grass, plenty of buffalo.

In summer it is almost as good as Crow country,

but in winter it is cold; the grass is gone

and there is no salt weed for the horses.

Arapooish, Chief of the Crows

First snowfall at St. Mary Lake, Glacier National Park, Montana.

Larch trees in October, Glacier National Park.

A little farther below was Dry Point,

so called because of the whitened tree trunks

covering the ground. Some were still erect;

some had fallen or were being supported by others.

This melancholy sight, coming right after the flowers,

recalled the paintings of Poussin

in which playing shepherds are represented.

Near them is a gravestone on which

are inscribed the words:"And I was a shepherd, too."

Nicolas Point, S.J.
A Journey on a Barge Down the Missouri

Clearing storm, Flathead Lake, Montana.

Bighorn Canyon, Montana.

Clearing storm, Red Rock Lakes National Wildlife Refuge, Montana.

Flathead River looking east, Polson, Montana.

Absaroka Range, Paradise Valley, Montana.

Sunset on the Mission Mountains,
St. Ignatius, Montana.

Common merganser, Bighorn Lake, Wyoming.

American avocet, Freezeout Lake, Montana.

following pages:
Mountain goat at Logan Pass,
Glacier National Park, Montana.

Black bear near Apikuni Falls, Glacier National Park, Montana.

Waterfall, Yellowstone National Park, Montana.

Lewis River, Yellowstone National Park, Montana.

Yellowstone River at Grand View Point,
Yellowstone National Park, Montana.

62

Great Fountain Geyser, Yellowstone National Park, Montana.

Think of Yellowstone in winter,

seven thousand seven hundred feet in elevation

at the lake, the nighttime lows thirty and forty below,

snows a dozen feet in depth, and the hot sulfur springs

boiling up, the grass still green beside them, down there

in the warm enclosure with the drifted snow

high above your head.

From the Introduction

Morning Glory Pool, Yellowstone National Park, Montana.

Minerva Terrace, Mammoth Hot Springs,
Yellowstone National Park, Montana.

67

Upper Geyser Basin, Yellowstone National Park.

Inspiration Point, Yellowstone National Park, Montana.

Think of early spring, bison wandering

through the mist near the steaming river

where the trumpeter swans

glide on glassy ponds.

From the Introduction

Geyser fog, Yellowstone National Park, Montana.

Lower Geyser Basin in March, Yellowstone National Park, Montana.

Running coyote in Hayden Valley, Yellowstone National Park.

Coyote in Hayden Valley, Yellowstone National Park, Montana.

Bugling elk, Yellowstone National Park.

Cottonwood tree, Flathead Valley, Montana.

Sunrise at erupting Castle Geyser, near Old Faithful,
Yellowstone National Park, Wyoming.

Smoke from forest fire over the Teton Mountains, Grand Teton National Park, Wyoming.

Absaroka Range, Montana.

Geyser snow, Yellowstone National Park, Montana.

Trumpeter swan on the Madison River, Yellowstone National Park.

Sunset on Jackson Lake, Grand Teton National Park, Wyoming.

Sunset at Oxbow Bend, Grand Teton National Park.

following pages:
Blue dusk, Grand Teton National Park.

As the sun set in a light haze, it exchanged the gold of its fire for the color of rubies. Above it, and outlined sharply against a blue background, a formation of clouds tinged with purple, blue, and violet hung like drapery. A row of beautiful trees cast their shadows to the middle of the river.

What was the crew doing in the presence of this rich coloring?

While the men drove our barges forward like so many chariots racing for a prize,

their wives and children sang hymns in honor of the Queen of Angels.

Never had the wilderness heard the like.

Nicolas Point, S.J.
A Journey on a Barge Down the Missouri

From the plain he could look down on the wooded valley of the
lower Teton. Magpies cried from down there, and a crow called,
sounding like a hoarse whisper against the wind that flowed
out of the northeast. Up on the plain, ground larks flitted from
under his horse's feet and jackass rabbits leaped out of hiding
and went bounding away, stopping to look after a while, their
front feet held up dainty and their coats already turned from
snow-white to dirty gray.

Spring was coming even if the weather didn't know it.

A week of good weather and the cottonwoods would bust

their buttons and the diamond willow run out leaves

as narrow as snakes' tongues, and at sundown a man

would hear the killdeer crying.

A.B. Guthrie, Jr., The Big Sky

Mt. Moran, Grand Teton National Park, Wyoming.

Devils Tower, Devils Tower National Monument, Wyoming.

Sawtooth Mountains, Stanley, Idaho.

preceding pages:
Star trails at Devils Tower, Devils Tower National Monument, Wyoming.

Craters of the Moon National Monument, Idaho.

From time to time he looked up from the book to roll on his side

and stare out across the coulee, across the barren plains

pimpled with gopher mounds and bitten with fire

and haired with dusty, woolly grass. Apparently as flat as a table,

the land sloped imperceptibly to the south, so that nothing interfered

with his view of the ghostly mountains, looking higher now

as the heat increased. Between his eyes and that smoky outline

sixty miles away the heat waves rose writhing like fine wavy hair.

Wallace Stegner, Big Rock Candy Mountain

Big Southern Butte. Arco. Idaho.

Bruneau Dunes State Park, Idaho.

Galloping horses, Polson, Montana.

Westward lay the Goosebill, long and low; northward the Sweetgrass Hills on the Canadian border, crowned with snow; behind us the Bear Paws made a jagged line against the sky; far to the south in the blue distance loomed the Highwoods. The sun shone on the grass sparkling with raindrops; the wild sweet peas nodded their yellow heads in friendly greeting. As I looked across the rolling expanse of prairie, fired with the beauty of a Montana sunset, I sent up a little prayer of thanksgiving from my heart for this, our very first home. Only a rectangle of prairie sod, raw and untouched by the hand of man, but to us it was a kingdom.

Pearl Price Robertson, Homestead Days in Montana

Old barn near Mission Mountains, Pablo, Montana.

That sense of separation can overwhelm you. Life in the northern Rockies
or on plains often seems to go on in a way not much connected to the doings
of the so-called "Great World." Ambitious young people leave early and never
go home for more than a few days at Christmas. Many of the people who stay
develop a deep mistrust of anything happening beyond their emotional
horizon. It is a way of being dysfunctional.

From the Introduction

Church, Lennep, Montana.

Oat field, Hailey, Idaho.

Hay field, Gannett, Idaho.

At the time of our marriage, four years before, there was nothing we wanted
so much as a home and a baby. We had no capital other than our love
for each other—very much of that—youth, inexperience, unshaken faith
in the future, a willingness to work. The home always came first in our plans
and was as beautiful as any dream home could be, with wide lawns, gardens,
and orchards, great barns and fertile fields—a farm built up out of the raw

land by the work of our own hands, a place to create beauty, to build projects, to change visions to reality; a haven and a refuge never to be completed throughout the years—we did not wish ever to come to the place where we could sit down with folded hands, saying, "It is finished; there is nothing more we can add."

Pearl Price Robertson, Homestead Days in Montana

Strip farming, Bynum, Montana.

Mountain bluebird, Ronan, Montana.

Spring foal, Bellevue, Idaho.

Schoolhouse on the range, West Yellowstone, Montana.

Silos, Conrad, Montana.

Canola field, Moscow, Idaho.

Sunflowers, Denton, Montana.

Rodeo, Wilsall, Montana.

Calf roping, Big Timber Rodeo, Montana.

following pages:
Round-up, Theodore Roosevelt National Park,
North Dakota.

Roadside poppies, Moscow, Idaho.

Strip farming, Cut Bank, Montana.

Farmhouse, Lewiston, Idaho.

Barn, near Lewiston, Idaho.

Sheep after June shearing, Red Lodge, Montana.

Boats at Lake McDonald, Glacier National Park, Montana.

Flyfishing the Boise River, Boise, Idaho.

Schoolhouse, Melville, Montana.

I loved the prairie, even while I feared it. God's country, the old-timers called it.
There is something about it which gets a man—or a woman. I feared its
relentlessness, its silence, and its sameness, even as I loved the tawny spread
of its sun-drenched ridges, its shimmering waves of desert air, the terrific sweep
of the untrammeled wind, burning starts in a midnight sky. Still in my dreams
I can feel the force of that wind, and hear its mournful wail around my shack
in the lonely hours of the night. . . .

Pearl Price Robertson, Homestead Days in Montana

Great Plains church, Melville, Montana.

June oats, Hailey, Idaho.

Grand Prismatic Pool, Yellowstone National Park, Montana.

138

St. Mary Lake, Glacier National Park, Montana.

Grain elevator, Wilsall, Montana.

The vast dry land farming country locals call the "Golden Triangle,"
enormous strips of fallow ground and wheatland which run over the plains
to the horizon, and on, begins north of Great Falls. Distances between
the little towns clustered at the foot of the towering grain elevators on the
"high-line" along the Great Northern tracks were dictated by concerns
about getting the crops to market.

This is the land of windbreaks beside white-painted farmsteads,
enormous four-wheel-drive diesel tractors and land-poor millionaires
with serious cash flow problems (a viable wheat farm on these plains
is worth a million anyway).

From the Introduction

Springtime, Big Timber, Montana.

Spring wheat, Conrad, Montana.

Out on those plains we find ourselves wondering about the rewards of freedom which led people to stick it out through blistering summers and blizzard winters, raising children on places where the nearest doctor was may be fifty snow-drifted miles away.

From the Introduction

146

Grain elevator, Choteau, Montana.

following pages:
Teton Village, Jackson Hole, Wyoming.

147

Bull moose at Oxbow Bend,
Grand Teton National Park, Wyoming.

We have seen many Elks Swimming the river, and they look almost the size of a well-grown mule. They stared at us, were fired at, at an enormous distance, it is true, and yet stood still. These animals are abundant beyond belief hereabouts. We have seen much remarkable handsome scenery...

John James Audubon, The Missouri River Journals, 1843

preceding pages:
Moon over Jackson, Wyoming.

Sunset at Wind Canyon,
Theodore Roosevelt National Park, North Dakota.

Sunset, Polson, Montana.

East Flattop Mountain, Glacier National Park, Montana.

Canola field, Moscow, Idaho.

Mule deer and fawn near Many Glacier, Glacier National Park, Montana.

Horse barn, Wilsall, Montana.

following pages:
Sunset on Gallatin Range,
Emigrant, Montana.

Spring colts. Highwood. Montana.

Wheat harvesting, Ethridge, Montana.

Rodeo bulls, Big Timber, Montana

By the 1890s the buffalo were
mostly gone from the plains.
The Crow warrior Two Leggings said,
"Nothing happened after that. We just
lived....There is nothing more to tell."

From the Introduction

Bison skull,
Theodore Roosevelt National Park,
North Dakota.

Bighorn Canyon, Montana.

Big Sky Country is truly "The Last Best Place," a land where it is still possible
to walk down the road and see only field, mountain, and sky, where the air is fresh,
the water is clean, and wildlife is all about. I wanted to capture this landscape
on film before it changed, and I am grateful to the people of Big Sky who have
preserved this paradise and shared it with me.

This book owes its life to many fine folk who were instrumental in making it happen:
Bill Black, my friend and collaborator who gave me my first assignment in
Big Sky Country; Tom Kennedy and Carol Enquist at *National Geographic*, who
gave me two more assignments to keep me there; my long-time picture editor,
Bobbie Baker Burrows, and *Life* magazine, which supplied the film and processing;
and Victor Bjornberg of *Travel Montana*, who gave me the wheels to put on
countless miles looking for perfection.

I am grateful for the support of Rizzoli in bringing the project to fruition and
particularly to Elizabeth White, who oversaw the editing and production, and to
David Larkin, the designer whose vision and insight brought the book into being.

Finally I must thank my wife, Gae, whose patience and generous spirit have been my
strength and my freedom, and my children, Peter, Caely, and Colin, whose love,
enthusiasm, and countless smiles have made my home a joyous place to come back to.

Michael Melford